LAUGH AND LEARN
Persian Idioms

Nazanin Mirsadeghi

Illustrations By: Maurice Gabry

Mirsadeghi, Nazanin
Laugh and Learn Persian Idioms (Farsi- English Bi-lingual Edition)/Nazanin Mirsadeghi

Illustrations by: Maurice Gabry
Editor: Molly Singleton-Coyne

ISBN-10: 1939099412
ISBN-13: 978-1-939099-41-9

Published by Bahar Books, White Plains, New York

PREFACE

Idioms are phrases in which the overall meaning differs from the literal meaning of its component. This makes idioms fun to hear, learn and use. By using idioms in daily conversations, one can convey a sense of humor, be more effective in making an argument, successfully grab the attention of listeners, and demonstrate a higher level of mastery of a language.

Most languages are rich in idioms and Persian is no exception. This book is an illustrated collection of 30 Persian idioms that you could learn and use in your daily conversations in Persian. Each idiom is presented with the "literal" translation in English to help you memorize the component parts. In addition, the "figurative" definition is given to communicate the true meaning of the idiom. Finally, an example in Persian with its English translation is provided to help you gain better understanding of the usage of the idiom in daily conversations. The transliteration of the idioms and related examples are also provided in this book.

To make the learning process fun, each idiom is accompanied by a graphic illustration, which is based on the "literal" translation of the idiom, rather its "figurative" definition. This will help you visualize the component parts of each idiom and will speed up your learning process. Also, in the beginning of the book, a brief overview of the Persian alphabet and the pronunciation of the Persian letters have been provided.

Pronouncing Persian Letters

ă like the **"a"** in arm	‍آ – ا *
b like the **"b"** in boy	ب – بـ
p like the **"p"** in play	پ – پـ
t like the **"t"** in tree	ت – تـ
s like the **"s"** in sun	ث – ثـ
j like the **"j"** in jam	ج – جـ
č like the **"ch"** in child	چ – چـ
h like the **"h"** in hotel	ح – حـ
ǩ like **"ch"** in the German word *bach*, or Hebrew word *smach*.	خ – خـ
d like the **"d"** in door	د
z like the **"z"** in zebra	ذ
r like the **"r"** in rabbit	ر
z like the **"z"** in zebra	ز
ž like the **"z"** in zwago	ژ

s like the "s" in sun	س – ﺳ
š like the "sh" in shell	ش – ﺷ
s like the "s" in sun	ص – ﺻ
z like the "z" in zebra	ض– ﺿ
t like the "t" in tree	ط
z like the "z" in zebra	ظ
' is a glottal stop, like between the syllables of "uh-oh".	ع – ﻋ – ﻌ
ğ like the "r " in French word *merci*	غ – ﻏ – ﻐ
f like the "f " in fall	ف – ﻓ
ğ like the "r" in French word *merci*	ق – ﻗ
k like the "k" in kite	ک – ﻛ
g like the "g" in game	گ – ﮔ
l like the "l" in lost	ل – ﻟ
m like the "m" in master	م – ﻣ
n like the "n" in night	ن – ﻧ
v like the "v" in van	و

o like the **"o"** in ocean	و
On some occasions, it has no sound and becomes silent.	و
u like the **"u"** in sure	* او – و
h like the **"h"** in hotel	ه – ـهـ – ـه – ﻩ
e like the **"e"** in element	ـه – ﻩ
y like the **"y"** in yellow	یـ – ی
i like the **"ee"** in need	* ایـ – یـ – ی – ای

    * long vowels

a like the **"a"** in animal	** آ – ٰ
o like the **"o"** in ocean	** أ – ٗ
e like the **"e"** in element	** ا – ٖ

    ** short vowels

Arabic Signs

Represents doubled consonants.	ّ
' is a glottal stop, like between the syllables of "uh-oh".	ء
an like "an" in the "can"	ً

Persian Letters with the Same Pronunciation

t like the "t" in tree	تـ – ت
	ط
ğ like the "r" in French word *merci*	قـ – ق
	غـ – ـغـ – غ
h like the "h" in hotel	حـ – ح
	هـ – ـهـ – ـه – ه
s like the "s" in sun	ثـ – ث
	سـ – س
	صـ – ص
z like the "z" in zebra	ذ
	ز
	ض
	ظ

Names Given to Persian Letters

alef	آ – ا
be	ب – بـ
pe	پ – پـ
te	ت – تـ
se	ث – ثـ
jim	ج – جـ
če	چ – چـ
he	ح – حـ
ke	خ – خـ
dăl	د
zăl	ذ
re	ر
ze	ز
že	ژ
sin	س – سـ
šin	ش – شـ

săd	صـ - ص
zăd	ضـ - ض
tă	ط
ză	ظ
eyn	عـ - ـعـ - ـع - ع
ğeyn	غـ - ـغـ - ـغ - غ
fe	فـ - ف
ğăf	قـ - ق
kăf	کـ - ک
găf	گـ - گ
lăm	لـ - ل
mim	مـ - م
noon	نـ - ن
văv	و
he	هـ - ـهـ - ـه - ه
ye	یـ - ی

LAUGH AND LEARN

Persian Idioms

سَرِ کسی کُلاه گُذاشتَن

/sa.re- ka.si- ko.lăh- go.zăš.tan/

Literal Translation: to put a hat on someone's head

Figurative Definition: to scam someone, to rip someone off

فُروشَنده گُفت که این گَردَنبَند از طَلای خالصِ است.

باوَرَم نِمی شَوَد که سَرَم کُلاه گُذاشت !

/fo.ru.šan.de- goft- ke- in- gar.dan.band- az- ta.lă.ye- kă.les- ast/
/bă.va.ram- ne.mi.ša.vad- ke- sa.ram- ko.lăh- go.zăšt/

The salesman said this necklace is made of pure gold.
I can't believe he ripped me off.

Yes! He put a hat on my head!

زیرِ بَغَلِ کسی هِندَوانه گُذاشتَن

/zi.re- ba.ğa.le- ka.si- hen.da.vă.ne- go.zăš.tan/

Literal Translation: to put watermelons under someone's arm

Figurative Definition: to flatter someone

اینقَدر زیرِ بَغَل رَئیسَت هِندَوانه نَگُذار، چون فایِده ای نَدارَد.

اگر بِخواهَد اِخراجَت کُنَد، می کُنَد.

/in.ğadr- zi.re- ba.ğa.le- ra.' i.sat- hen.da.vă.ne- nago.zăr- čon-
fă.ye.de.i- na.dă.rad/
/agar- be.kă.had- ek.ră.jat- ko.nad- mi.ko.nad/

Stop flattering your boss because it is useless.
If he wants to fire you, he will.

Don't put watermelons under his arms!

از خَرِ شِیطان پایین آمَدَن

/az- ǩa.re- šey.tăn- pă.yin- ă.ma.dan/

Literal Translation: *to dismount from the devil's donkey*

Figurative Definition: to be very stubborn

خانه‌ی ما کنارِ بُزُرگراه است.

کاشکی شوهَرِ من از خَرِ شِیطان پایین می آمَد و به
فُروشَش رِضایَت می داد.

/ǩă.ne.ye- mă- ke.nă.re- bo.zorg.răh- ast/
/kăš.ki- šo.ha.re- man- az- ǩa.re- šey.tăn- pă.yin- mi.ă.mad- va-
be- fo.ru.šaš- re.ză.yat- mi.dăd/

Our house is right next to the highway. I wish my
husband would stop being so stubborn and agree to sell it.

He doesn't want to dismount from the
devil's donkey!

از این گوش شنیدَن و از آن گوش دَر کردَن *

/az- in- guš- še.ni.dan- va- az- ăn- guš- dar- kar.dan/

Literal Translation: to hear from one ear and let it go out from another ear.

Figurative Definition: to pay no attention to someone's advice.

* Similar to the English idiom: it goes in one ear and comes out the other.

مادَر بُزُرگِ من دَستورِ دُکتُرَش را از این گوش می شنَوَد و از آن گوش دَر می کُنَد.

به جای اِستِراحَت، هَر روز می رَوَد اِسکی روی یَخ !

/mă.dar.bo.zor.ge- man- das.tu.re- dok.to.raš- ră- az- in- guš-
mi.še.na.vad- va- az- ăn- guš- dar- mi.ko.nad/
/be.jă.ye- es.te.ră.hat- har- ruz- mi.ra.vad- es.ki.ye- ru.ye- yaǩ/

My grandmother doesn't pay any attention to her doctor's order.
Instead of resting, she goes ice skating every day!

Granny, you hear it with one ear and let it
go out from the other!

دَست خود نَبودَن

/das.te- ǩod- na.bu.dan/

Literal Translation: *to not be one's own hand*

Figurative Definition: to be unable to help oneself, to be unable to resist doing something or control one's behavior

من عاشِقِ گیلاسَم؛ اگر گیلاس بِبینَم، بایَد هَمه اش را بِخورَم.

دَستِ خودَم نیست !

/man- 'ǎ.še.ǧe- gi.lǎ.sam- a.gar- gi.lǎs- be.bi.nam- bǎ.yad-
ha.me.aš- rǎ- be.ǩo.ram/
/das.te- ǩo.dam- nist/

I love cherries. If I see some, I have to have them all.
I just can't help myself!

Sorry! This is not my own hand!

بَرایِ کسی پاپوش دُرُست کردَن

/ba.rǎ.ye- ka.si- pǎ.puš- do.rost- kar.dan/

Literal Translation: to make footwear for someone

Figurative Definition: to set someone up

پُلیس اِسکِناس هایِ دُزدی را در خانه‌ی هَمسایه‌ی من پِیدا کرده است، امّا هَمسایه ام می گویَد که بی گُناه است. اِدّعا می کُنَد که بَرایَش پاپوش دُرُست کرده اند !

/po.lis- es.ke.nǎs.hǎ.ye- doz.di- rǎ- dar- kǎ.ne.ye- ham.sǎ.ye.ye- man-
pey.dǎ- kar.de- ast- am.mǎ- ham.sǎ.ye.am- mi.gu.yad- ke- bi.go.nǎh- ast/
/ed.de.'ǎ- mi.ko.nad- ke- ba.rǎ.yaš- pǎ.puš- do.rost- kar.de.and/

The police have found the stolen money in my
neighbor's house; but my neighbor says he is innocent.
He claims that they have set him up!

Officer! I didn't rob the bank.
They made footwear for me!

دَسته گُل به آب دادَن

/das.te- gol- be- ăb- dă.dan/

Literal Translation: *to throw the flower bouquet in the water*

Figurative Definition: to make a big mistake, to mess up

ما توی تاریکی نِشَسته ایم چون شوهَرَم باز هَم دَسته گُل به آب داده است! یادَش رَفته است قَبضِ بَرق را پَرداخت کُنَد!

/mă- tu.ye- tă.ri.ki- ne.šas.te.im- čon- šo.ha.ram- băz- ham-
das.te- gol- be- ăb- dă.de- ast/
/yă.daš- raf.te- ast- ğab.ze- barğ- ră- par.dăǩt- ko.nad/

We are sitting in the dark because my husband has
messed up again!
He has forgotten to pay the electric bills!

I can't believe this! You threw the flower
bouquet in the water again!

سَر به سَرِ کسی گُذاشتَن

/sar- be- sa.re- ka.si- go.zaš.tan/

Literal Translation: to put one's head on someone else's head

Figurative Definition: to kid someone or trick them into believing something

اینقَدر سَر به سَرِ بَرادرَت نَگُذار.

زیرِ تَختَش لولوخورخوره نیست !

/in.ğadr- sar- be- sa.re- ba.ră.da.rat- na.go.zăr/
/zi.re- tak.taš- lu.lu.ǩor.ǩo.re- nist/

Stop kidding your brother!
There is no monster under his bed!

26

My brother puts his head on my head all the time!

پول ِ کسی را خوردَن

/pu.le- ka.si- rǎ- ǩor.dan/

Literal Translation: *to eat someone's money*

Figurative Definition: to embezzle someone's money

من بِهِشان اِعتِماد کردَم و پولَم را به دَست ِ شان سِپُردَم.
آنها هَم پولَم را خوردَند !

/man- be.he.šǎn- eʻ.te.mǎd- kar.dam- va- pu.lam- rǎ- be-
das.te.šǎn- se.por.dam/
/ǎn.hǎ- ham- pu.lam- rǎ- ǩor.dand/

I trusted them with my money.
They just took it!

I thought you were my friends!
You ate my money!

زیرِ پای کسیِ نِشَستَن

/zi.re- păye- ka.si- ne.šas.tan/

Literal Translation: to sit under someone's feet (legs)

Figurative Definition: to tempt someone to do something

بَرادَرَم عاشِقِ کادیلاکَش بود و اصلاً قَصد نَداشت
بِفُروشَدَش؛ دوستَش زیرِ پایَش نِشَست !

/ba.ră.da.ram- ʻă.še.ğe- kă.di.lă.kaš- bud- va- as.lan- ğasd-
na.dăšt- be.fo.ru.ša.daš- dus.taš- zi.re- pă.yaš- ne.šast/

My brother loved his Cadillac and had no intention
of selling it. His friend tempted him!

I didn't want to sell it!
You sat under my legs!

دو پایِ خود را در یِک کَفش کردَن

/do- pǎ.ye- ǩod- rǎ- dar- yek- kafš- kar.dan/

Literal Translation: to put both feet in one shoe

Figurative Definition: to insist on wanting to do something despite advice against it.

نمی دانَم چه کار کُنَم؛ پِسَرَم دو پایَش را در یِک کَفش کرده است و می خواهَد بِرَوَد صَخره نَوَردی !

/ne.mi.dǎ.nam- če- kǎr- ko.nam- pe.sa.ram- do- pǎ.yaš- rǎ- dar- yek- kafš- kar.de- ast- va- mi.ǩǎ.had- be.ra.vad- saǩ.re.na.var.di/

I don't know what to do;
My son insists on going rock climbing!

He has put two feet in one shoe and wants
to do it!

جایِ کسی را خالی کردَن

/jă.ye- ka.si- ră- ǩă.li- kar.dan/

Literal Translation: *to empty someone's place*

Figurative Definition: to think of someone in their absence
and wish they were present

ما دیروز توی مِهمانی جایِ تو را خِیلی خالی کردیم !

/mă- di.ruz- tu.ye- meh.mă.ni- jă.ye- to- ră- ǩey.li- ǩă.li- kar.dim/

We thought of you a lot at the party yesterday and
wished you were there with us!

We always empty your place when we get together!

دِل به دَریا زدَن

/del- be- dar.yă- za.dan/

Literal Translation: to throw one's heart into the sea

Figurative Definition: to take the plunge, to try something risky

می دانِستَم که با من اِزدِواج نَخواهَد کرد، امّا باز هَم دِل به دَریا زَدَم و از او خواستِگاری کردَم.

/mi.dă.nes.tam- ke- bă- man- ez.de.văj- na.kă.had- kard- am.mă-
băz- ham- del- be- dar.yă- za.dam- va- az- u- kăs.te.gă.ri- kar.dam/

I knew she wouldn't marry me, but I took the plunge
and proposed anyway.

I decided to throw my heart into the sea!

دَست از سَرِ کسی بَرداشتَن

/dast- az- sa.re- ka.si- bar.dăš.tan/

Literal Translation: to remove one's hand from someone's head

Figurative Definition: to leave someone alone

اینقَدر نِق نَزَن !

دَست از سَرِ شوهَرِ بیچاره ات بَردار !

/in.ğadr- neğ- na.zan/
/dast- az- sa.re- šo.ha.re- bi.čă.re.at- bar.dăr/

Stop nagging so much!
Leave your poor husband alone!

Remove your hand from my head,
sweetheart!

دَست و پای ِخود را گُم کردَن

/dast- va- pă.ye- ǩod- ră- gom- kar.dan/

Literal Translation: to lose one's hand and leg

Figurative Definition: to panic

وَقتی پُلیس از او گُواهینامه ی رانَندِگی اش را خواست،

دَست و پایَش را گُم کرد.

/vağ.ti- po.lis- az- u- go.vă.hi.nă.me.ye- ră.nan.de.gi.aš- ră- ǩăst-
dast- va- pă.yaš- ră- gom- kard/

When the police asked for his driver's license, he
panicked.

Sir! Please don't lose your hands and legs;
I'm just asking for your driver's license.

دلِ کسی بَرای کسی تَنگ شُدَن

/de.le- ka.si- ba.ră.ye- ka.si- tang- šo.dan/

Literal Translation: to feel one's heart tightening for someone

Figurative Definition: to miss someone

دو ماه است نامزَدَم را نَدیده ام.

دِلَم بَرایَش خِیلی تَنگ شُده است !

/do- măh- ast- năm.za.dam- ră- na.di.de.am/
/de.lam- ba.ră.yaš- ḱey.li- tang- šo.de- ast/

I haven't seen my fiancé in two months.
I've missed him so much!

My heart is so tightened for you, my love!

بیخِ ریشِ کسی ماندَن

/bi.ke- ri.še- ka.si- măn.dan/

Literal Translation: to sit at the bottom of someone's beard

Figurative Definition: to be a burden on someone, to be taken care of by someone else for a long time

پسَرخاله ام بیکار شُده است و با من زِندِگی می کُنَد.

نِمی دانَم تا کِی بیخِ ریشِ من خواهَد ماند.

/pe.sar.kă.le.am- bi.kăr- šo.de- ast- va- bă- man- zen.de.gi-
mi.ko.nad/
/ne.mi.da.nam- tă- key- bi.ke- ri.še- man- kă.had- mănd/

My cousin has lost his job and he is living with me now. I don't know how long I will be stuck with him.

Yes! He is sitting at the bottom of my beard!

دَست کسی نَمَک نَداشتَن

/das.te- ka.si- na.mak- na.dăš.tan/

Literal Translation: one's hand has no salt

Figurative Definition: (for one's generosity) to go
unappreciated all the time

بَرایِ هَمسَرَم ماشینِ نو خَریدَم، امّا از من تَشَکُّر هَم نَکرد !
دَستَم نَمَک نَدارَد !

/ba.ră.ye- ham.sa.ram- mă.ši.ne- no- ǩa.ri.dam- am.mă- az- man-
ta.šak.kor- ham- na.kard/
/das.tam- na.mak- na.dă.rad/

I bought a new car for my wife, but she didn't even
thank me!
My kindness never gets recognized!

What can I say, my hand has no salt!

سِبیلِ کسی را چَرب کردَن

/se.bi.le- ka.si- rǎ- čarb- kar.dan/

Literal Translation: to grease someone's mustache

Figurative Definition: to bribe someone

بَرادَرَم می گویَد تا سِبیلِ رَئیسِ بانک را چَرب نَکُنَم، وامَم دُرُست نَخواهَد شُد.

/ba.rǎ.da.ram- mi.gu.yad- tǎ- se.bi.le- ra.' i.se- bǎnk- rǎ- čarb- na.ko.nam- vǎ.mam- do.rost- na.ǩǎ.had- šod/

My brother says my bank loan won't be approved unless I bribe the bank manager.

I had no choice but to grease his mustache.

کَف دَست خود را بو نَکردَن

/ka.fe- das.te- ǩod- rǎ- bu- na.kar.dan/

Literal Translation: to not smell the palm of one's hand

Figurative Definition: to not have predicted something

ماشینَم را به دوستَم قَرض دادَم، امّا کَف دَستَم را بو نَکرده
بودَم که می زَنَدَش به دِرَخت !

/mǎ.ši.nam- rǎ- be- dus.tam- ǧarz- dǎ.dam- am.mǎ- ka.fe- das.tam-
rǎ- bu- na.kar.de- bu.dam- ke- mi.za.na.daš- be- de.raǩt/

I lent my car to my friend but I didn't expect him to
drive it into a tree!

I didn't smell the palm of my hand that this
could happen!

زَبانِ کسی مو دَر آوَردَن

/za.bă.ne- ka.si- mu- dar- ă.var.dan/

Literal Translation: *to grow hair on one's tongue*

Figurative Definition: to be tired of repeating something

از بَس به بَچّه هایَم گُفتَم اُتاقِ شان را تَمیز کُنَند، زَبانَم

مو دَر آوَرد !

/az- bas- be- bač.če.hă.yam- gof.tam- o.tă.ğe.šăn- ră- ta.miz-
ko.nand- za.bă.nam- mu- dar- ă.vard/

I'm so tired of asking my kids over and over to clean
their room.

Believe me, my tongue has grown hair!

موی دَماغِ کسی شُدَن

/mu.ye- da.mă.ğe- ka.si- šo.dan/

Literal Translation: *to become someone's nasal hair*

Figurative Definition: to annoy or bother someone

آنقَدر موی دَماغِ رَئیسَم می شَوَم تا حُقوقَم را بالا بِبَرَد.

/ăn.ğadr- mu.ye- da.mă.ğe- ra.' i.sam- mi.ša.vam- tă- ho.ğu.ğam- ră- bă.lă- be.ba.rad/

I'll keep getting in my boss's face until he gives me a raise.

It's been six months since I have become a hair in his nose!

كَلّهی کسی سوت کشیدَن

/kal.le.ye- ka.si- sut- ke.ši.dan/

Literal Translation: *one's head to whistle*

Figurative Definition: (one's mind) to be blown, to be extremely surprised

وَقتی گُفتَند خانه شان را چَند خَریده اند، کَلّه ام سوت کِشید !

/vağ.ti- gof.tand- kă.ne.šăn- ră- čand- ka.ri.de.and- kal.le.am- sut- ke.šid/

When they said how much they paid for their house, it blew my mind!

It was so expensive, my head whistled!

مُخِ کسی را خوردَن

/mo.ǩe- ka.si- rǎ- ǩor.dan/

Literal Translation: *to eat someone's brain*

Figurative Definition: to drive someone crazy by talking non-stop

زَنی که توی هَواپیما کِنارَم نِشَسته بود، در طول پَرواز مُخَم را خورد.

/za.ni- ke- tu.ye- ha.vǎ.pey.mǎ- ke.nǎ.ram- ne.šas.te- bud- dar-
tu.le- par.vǎz- mo.ǩam- rǎ- ǩord/

The woman, who was sitting next to me on the plane, drove me crazy by talking non-stop during the flight.

Lady! Have some mercy on me!
You are eating my brain!

شِکَمِ خود را صابون زَدَن

/še.ka.me- kod- ră- să.bun- za.dan/

Literal Translation: *to soap one's stomach*

Figurative Definition: to expect something to happen in one's favor

پِسَرَم شِکَمَش را صابون زَده است که این تابِستان به دیزنی‌لَند می رَویم.

/pe.sa.ram- še.ka.maš- ră- să.bun- za.de- ast- ke- in- tă.bes.tăn- be- dis.ni.land- mi.ra.vim/

My son is very much hoping that we go to Disneyland this summer.

I am soaping my belly for the summer, mom!

چَشم و چِراغِ کسی بودَن

/čašm- va- če.ră.ğe- ka.si- bu.dan/

Literal Translation: *to be someone's eye and lamp*

Figurative Definition: to be very dear to someone, to be the light of someone's life

این دُختَر بَچّه، چَشم و چِراغِ مادَرَش است !

/in- doǩ.tar.bač.če- čašm- va- če.ră.ğe- mă.da.raš- ast/

This little girl means the world to her mother!

You are my eye and lamp, dear!

توی کارِ کسی موش دَواندَن

/tu.ye- kă.re- ka.si- muš- da.văn.dan/

Literal Translation: to run mice through someone's business

Figurative Definition: to undermine someone's work

هَمکارِ من مُدام توی کارِ من موش می دَوانَد.
واقِعاً نِمی دانَم بایَد چه کار کُنَم !

/ham.kă.re- man- mo.dăm- tu.ye- kă.re- man- muš-
mi.da.vă.nad/
/vă.ğe.an- ne.mi.dă.nam- bă.yad- če- kăr- ko.nam/

My co-worker keeps undermining my work.
I really don't know what to do!

Hey pal, stop running mice through my business!

دَست کسی کَج بودَن

/das.te- ka.si- kaj- bu.dan/

Literal Translation: one's hand is crooked

Figurative Definition: to have a tendency to steal from other people

شِرکَتِ من هَر ماه پول از دَست می دَهَد.

فِکر می کُنَم حِسابدارَم دَستَش کَج است.

/šer.ka.te- man- har- măh- pul- az- dast- mi.da.had/
/fekr- mi.ko.nam- he.săb.dă.ram- das.taš- kaj- ast/

My company loses money every month.
I think my accountant might be stealing from me.

How dare you accusing me of having a crooked hand?

چَشمِ کسی آب نَخوردَن

/češ.me- ka.si- ăb- na.ǩor.dan/

Literal Translation: one's eye does not drink water

Figurative Definition: to be very skeptical of something

پِسَرَم قول داده است که دیگر با کسی دَعوا نَکُنَد،

امّا من چِشمَم اصلاً آب نِمی خورَد.

/pe.sa.ram- ğol- dă.de- ast- ke- di.gar- bă- ka.si- da'.vă-
na.ko.nad- am.mă- man- češ.mam- as.lan- ăb- ne.mi.ǩo.rad/

My son has promised me that he will not fight with anyone any more, but I'm very skeptical.

My eye does not drink water that you will change your behavior, kid!

* از خوشحالی سَر از پا نَشناختَن

/az- ǩoš.hǎ.li- sar- az- pǎ- na.še.nǎǩ.tan/

Literal Translation: to not recognize head from foot

Figurative Definition: to be extremely excited

* Similar to the English idiom: head over heels

پِسَرَم از خوشحالی سَر از پا نِمی شِناسَد چون من بَرایَش ماشین خَریده ام.

/pe.sa.ram- az- ǩoš.hǎ.li- sar- az- pǎ- ne.mi.še.nǎ.sad- čon- man-
ba.rǎ.yaš- mǎ.šin- ǩa.ri.de.am/

My son is so excited because I bought a car for him.

I am so excited that I don't recognize my
head from my foot!

Vocabulary

آ

to drink water	آب خوردن

ا

room	اتاق
to fire someone	اخراج کردن
to claim	ادّعا کردن
to lose	از دست دادن
to marry	ازدواج کردن
resting	استراحت
dollar bill	اسکناس
ice skating	اسکی روی یخ
no way	اصلاً
to trust	اعتماد کردن
if	اگر
but	امّا

ب

again	باز هم
to believe	باور کردن
must	باید

child	بچّه
brother	برادر
for	برای
highway	بزرگراه
to smell	بو کردن
instead of	به جای
to hand in	به دستِ کسی سپردن
poor	بیچاره
bottom	بیخ
unemployed	بیکار
innocent	بی گناه

پ

footwear	پاپوش
to dismount	پایین آمدن
to pay	پرداخت کردن
flight	پرواز
son	پسر
cousin (boy)	پسرخاله
policeman	پلیس
stolen money	پولِ دزدی
to find	پیدا کردن

ت

summer	تابستان

darkness	تاریکی
bed	تخت
to thank	تشکر کردن
to clean	تمیز کردن
to get tightened	تنگ شدن
inside/in	تویِ

to propose marriage	خواستگاری کردن
to want	خواستن
to eat	خوردن
joy	خوشحالی
very	خیلی

چ

lamp/light	چراغ
to grease	چرب کردن
eye	چشم
because	چون

د

to know	دانستن
tree	درخت
during	در طولِ
to let go out	در کردن
sea	دریا
hand	دست
order	دستور
flower bouquet	دسته گل
to fight	دعوا کردن
doctor	دکتر
heart/stomach	دل
to run	دواندن
friend	دوست
to see	دیدن
yesterday	دیروز

ح

accountant	حسابدار
to give someone a raise	حقوقِ کسی را بالا بردن

خ

pure	خالص
to empty	خالی کردن
house	خانه
donkey	خر
to buy	خریدن

ر

to consent	رضایت دادن
to go	رفتن
beard	ریش
boss	رئیس

ز

tongue	زبان
to live	زندگی کردن
under	زیرِ
under arm	زیرِ بغل

س

mustache	سبیل
head	سر
to whistle	سوت کشیدن

ش

company	شرکت
stomach	شکم
to recognize	شناختن
to hear	شنیدن
husband	شوهر
devil	شیطان

ص

soap	صابون
rock climbing	صخره نوردی

ط

gold	طلا

ع

to be in love	عاشق بودن

ف

to be effective	فایده داشتن
to sell	فروختن
selling	فروش
salesman	فروشنده
to think	فکر کردن

ق

electric bill	قبضِ برق
to lend	قرض دادن
to intend	قصد داشتن
to promise	قول دادن

ک

I wish	کاشکی
business/job	کار
to be crooked	کج بودن
someone	کسی
palm of hand	کف دستِ
shoe	کفش
hat	کلاه
head	کلّه
next to	کنارِ

م

grandmother	مادربزرگ
car	ماشین
to stay	ماندن
month	ماه
brain	مخ
all the time	مدام
to grow hair	مو درآوردن
mouse	موش
nasal hair	موی دماغ
party	مهمانی

گ

to put	گذاشتن
necklace	گردنبند
to say	گفتن
to lose	گم کردن
driver's license	گواهینامه‌ی رانندگی
ear	گوش
cherry	گیلاس

ن

fiancé	نامزد
to sit	نشستن
to nag	نق زدن
salt	نمک
new	نو

ل

monster	لولوخورخوره

و

really	واقعاً
loan	وام
when	وقتی

ه

every day	هر روز
neighbor	همسایه
spouse	همسر
co-worker	همکار
all	همه
watermelon	هندوانه
plane	هواپیما

ی

to learn	یاد گرفتن

Similar Titles

Essentials of
Persian Grammar
(Concepts & Exercises)

Nazanin Mirsadeghi

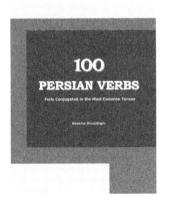

100
Persian Verbs
(Fully Conjugated in the Most Common Tenses)

Nazanin Mirsadeghi

1000 +
Most Useful
Persian Verbs

Nazanin Mirsadeghi

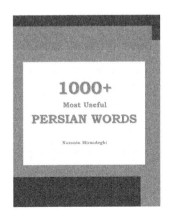

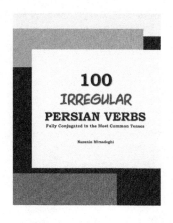

100
Irregular
Persian Verbs
(Fully Conjugated in the Most Common Tenses)
Nazanin Mirsadeghi

Persian Folktale

Once Upon a Time
(Seven Persian Folktales)
Meimanat Mirsadeghi (Zolghadr)

To Learn More About BAHAR BOOKS

Please Visit the Website:

www.baharbooks.com

Bahar Books

Printed by Amazon Italia Logistica S.r.l.
Torrazza Piemonte (TO), Italy